S0-CFA-605

ANIMAL SCAVENGERS
Jackals

Ypsilanti District Library
5577 Whittaker Road
Ypsilanti, MI 48197

SANDRA MARKLE

LERNER PUBLICATIONS COMPANY / MINNEAPOLIS

THE ANIMAL WORLD IS FULL OF
SCAVENGERS.

Scavengers are the cleanup crew who find and eat carrion (dead animals) in order to survive. Every day, animals are born and animals die. Without scavengers, the bodies of dead animals would rot away slowly. The decaying flesh would smell bad and take up space. It could also pollute water and attract flies and other disease-carrying insects. Fortunately, scavengers everywhere eat dead and dying animals before they have time to rot. *In the grasslands and dry deserts of Africa, black-backed jackals are part of the scavenger cleanup crew.*

It's October, and it's spring in Africa. The rainy season has just begun, but the land remains brown and dry. Food is scarce for wildebeest and other grazing animals. This is a hard time for the youngest and oldest animals. Weak animals may die or become easy prey for lions, spotted hyenas, and other predators. The carcasses provide plenty of food for jackals.

At dawn, while the air is still nighttime cool, the female black-backed jackal wakes up and stretches. She usually forages (searches for food) during the early morning, the evening, and into the night. These are the coolest parts of the day.

When the female stirs, her mate lifts his head and yawns. Then he gets up too. Like the female, he resembles a medium-sized dog with a pointed muzzle, big ears, and a very long bushy tail.

Jackals often behave like dogs too. Each time the mated jackals meet, they lick each other's ears and groom each other. Like other jackal pairs, they mate for life. Sometimes jackal pairs hunt and raise their young by themselves. Other times, as with this family, the young adult females from one litter of pups will stay to help raise the next litter.

The warm air is already steamy by the time the jackal family sets out to forage for food. The mated pair travels together. Each of the young adults goes off alone. They trot at about the same speed a human might jog.

Each jackal stops often to deposit scent markings. Jackals have scent glands near their tails that leave scent droplets with their urine. These personal markers announce to other jackals that this territory is already claimed. The family's territory is the area they know well and where they find their food. Leaving scent markers lets other jackals know they'll be attacked if they are caught feeding on the family's home turf.

From time to time, the jackals stop to sniff the air. Like dogs, jackals have a good sense of smell. They can detect odors as far away as one-half mile (nearly one kilometer). Their view of the world is shaped by what they smell as much as by what they see.

Jackals have sharp eyesight too. When the female black-backed spots vultures circling overhead, she heads in that direction. Her mate follows after her. The jackals know that vultures in the air mean carrion nearby on the ground. The pair uses their sharp sense of smell to lead them to the carrion. The vultures are already tearing into the body of the dead giraffe.

A lone male black-backed jackal is also feeding on the giraffe. He is in the pairs' territory. Male jackals usually attack intruding males, and females attack females. The paired male charges and body slams the intruding lone male. Growling and snapping, the intruder stands his ground. Ears back and tails lashing, the two males wrestle. Each tries to bite the other's throat. They separate and circle, snarling and snapping. Then the two males wrestle again. The fight continues until the intruder breaks away. His mouth gapes in a grin that shows he has submitted, or given up. The paired male lets the intruder escape. Black-backed jackal fights rarely end with serious injury.

Many more vultures arrive during the fight. They take over the carrion. Growling and nipping, the female jackal forces some of the vultures to take flight. Then the jackals each pick a spot at the giraffe carcass and dig in. Jackals don't have powerful jaws and can't crush bones. They don't have big strong teeth to rip open tough skin. So the jackals have to gnaw through the skin first. Then they peel the soft flesh from the bone and gulp it down.

The male pulls off a large chunk of the giraffe and carries it off. He digs a hole in the sand and buries the food to store it. The jackals may come back another day to dig up this food supply. Just as likely, another jackal or another scavenger may sniff it out and dig it up before the pair returns.

As the day heats up, the jackals head toward their den. Early in the rainy season, water is starting to flow into the dry rivers and streams. Jackals are adapted to the dry environment and can survive on the moisture they get from the flesh of carrion they eat. Sometimes they also eat plants, such as wild berries or the grass that's just sprouting. Still, jackals will drink when they get a chance. When the female black-backed comes to a stream, she wades in.

This is the last time the mother black-backed jackal will forage for a few days. Back at the den site, she crawls into the narrow entrance of an abandoned aardvark burrow. There she gives birth to the six pups that have been developing inside her for the past two months. The pups are tiny when they are born, and their eyes are closed. During the first three weeks of their lives, their mother will rarely leave them. While she guards and nurses the pups, her mate and her two young adult daughters will help take care of her. When they come back from a foraging trip, the adults will bring up some of the food in their stomachs for her to eat.

When a sudden thunderstorm hits, the den floods. The mother manages to carry only three of the pups to safety—a male and two females.

Nursing frequently, the jackal pups quickly grow bigger. By the time the pups are about three weeks old, the mother often leaves them alone. She joins the other adults to forage for food. It takes a lot of food to feed the rapidly growing pups. So the adult jackals spend a lot of time foraging. The pups are eating meat as well as nursing. So when the adults return, the pups come to them, whining to be fed. The partly digested meat the adults bring up for them is perfect jackal pup food.

When the mated pair track down a dead elephant, they hurry to join the spotted hyena that is already feeding. Usually a hyena would drive off any competition. It would make the jackals wait until it had finished eating. This time, though, there is plenty for everyone.

Another day the two young adult females spot a female Thomson's gazelle chasing away a golden jackal. The black-backed jackals see that the gazelle is defending her calf.

Before the mother gazelle can return, the jackals have killed the calf and are eating it. Black-backed jackals will eat whatever they can overpower, such as rodents and hares. Sometimes, like today, it can also be a baby gazelle.

At the den site, the pups play. One pup chases another and pounces on it. Sometimes one pup will ambush (surprise) another pup and then pounce on it. Most of these games end up in wrestling matches. While they play, the jackal pups are becoming strong and well coordinated.

Nosing through the grass, the little male's sharp senses pick up a rustling noise and a new smell. The pup discovers a frog. When the frog hops, the startled youngster pounces and tosses the frog into the air. The pup catches the frog and tosses it again. Finally, tired of the game, the little male gulps down his first kill.

By the time they are ten weeks old, the jackal pups have stopped nursing. They go along with the adults on foraging trips. By following the adults, they get to know the family's territory. The young male runs ahead. He has caught the scent of carrion and finds a dead wildebeest calf. He lifts his head and yowls to call the others.

But the wildebeest calf is the kill of a spotted hyena clan. The hyenas growl and hiss, warning the jackals that they'll defend their prey. Hyenas have strong teeth and a bone-crushing bite. So the jackals wait until the hyenas eat their fill. Then they dig into the scraps.

Before long, the young jackal male is spending more time foraging alone. When he's about eleven months old, he leaves his family. At first, he doesn't try to claim a territory. Instead, he forages in one area for a few days or for a few weeks. Then he travels on and looks for food in another area.

The young male usually eats carrion. It could be
the remains of a predator's kill or an
animal that has died. But he's
learned how to hunt too. When
he spots a mouse scurrying
across the ground, he
pounces on it and
gulps it down.

One day, the young black-backed jackal is an intruder in another male's territory. While the resident female watches, the resident male attacks. The two males wrestle, growling and snapping at each other.

The young black-backed male is smaller than the resident male and quickly gives up. To signal that he's giving up, the young male pulls his tail between his back legs and lowers his body close to the ground. The resident male backs off, and the younger male runs away.

The young male continues to roam. He grows bigger and stronger over time. He also becomes a more cunning scavenger, learning to follow lions or hyenas and waiting to eat their leftovers. He learns to find carrion by watching where vultures are circling. And he becomes better at chasing vultures away so that he can have a chance to feed.

The young male continues to forage and travel alone all winter. But during the spring, he meets a young black-backed female who is also foraging alone. The two mate, forming a pair bond that will last their lifetime. Then they claim a territory that isn't occupied by other black-backed jackals. Eventually they dig a den.

About two months later, the young female gives birth to three pups. This is her first litter, so she doesn't have any older pups to help her raise the young. A few weeks later, a spotted hyena kills two of the pups while the parents are away foraging for food. It will be easier for the pair to raise the one surviving pup to adulthood. Then the African grassland's jackal cleanup crew will be another generation stronger.

Looking Back

- Take another look at the jackals on pages 21, 28, and 33 and find out what sounds they're making. Jackals make soft chirping sounds to their young. They whine when stressed and growl at rivals. They may give a series of sharp barks to call the members of their family group together. They may also call to them by throwing their heads back and howling.

- Check out the jackal's ears on pages 5 and 15. Can you guess why it lays its ears flat against its head while competing for a meal?

- Look again at page 29 to see how jackals compare in size to one of their competitors, spotted hyenas? How might being smaller help jackals get a share of their rival's meals?

Glossary

CARRION: a dead animal that a scavenger eats

DEN: the female jackal uses a burrow as a birth den for her pups. This may be a burrow that another animal abandoned or that the parents dig themselves.

FAMILY: a group of jackals made up of a mated pair, any young from a previous litter, and any pups

FORAGE: to search for food

LITTER: a group of pups born at one time

PREDATOR: an animal that hunts and eats other animals to survive

PREY: an animal that a predator catches to eat

PUP: a young jackal

SCAVENGER: an animal that feeds on dead animals

SCENT: an animal's sense of smell, or an odor left behind by an animal

TERRITORY: another name for an animal's home range

Further Information

BOOKS

Estes, Richard Despard. *The Behavior Guide to African Mammals: Including Hoofed Mammals, Carnivores, Primates.* Berkeley: University of California Press, 1992. This encyclopedic book for older readers contains insights into the African ecosystem where jackals live.

Gentle, Victor. *Jackals: Wild Dogs.* Milwaukee: Gareth Stevens, 2002. This book describes the lives of these animals and how they raise their young.

Pringle, Laurence. *Jackal Woman: Exploring the World of Jackals.* New York: Atheneum, 1993. This book describes the life and behavior of jackals and the fieldwork of biologist Patricia Moehlman.

VIDEO

National Geographic's African Wildlife (National Geographic, 1997). This view of African wildlife in Namibia's Etosha National Park shows a wide range of wildlife and how they interact in a balanced ecosystem.

WEBSITES

African Wildlife Foundation. *Wildlives.* http://www.awf.org/wildlives/144. Find information about jackals, their characteristics, habitats, eating patterns, and more.

Siyabona Africa. *Jackal Sounds.* http://www.africatravel.co.za/africa_jackal_sounds.html. Listen to the sounds that jackals make.

Index

For Aaron Donaldson, in honor of his work with Hillview Christian School

The author would like to thank Nicola Jenner, PhD student researching black-backed jackals, co-supervised by Dr. Stephen Funk at the Institute of Zoology (Zoological Society London) and Dr. Jim Groombrige at the University of Kent, United Kingdom, and Dr. Jan Nel, University of Stellenbosch, Stellenbosch, South Africa, for sharing their expertise and enthusiasm. The author would also like to express a special thank-you to Skip Jeffery for his help and support during the creative process.

Photo Acknowledgments

The images in this book are used with the permission of: © Carol Polich/ Lonely Planet Images/Getty Images, p. 1; © Francesc Muntada/CORBIS, p. 3; © Richard Du Toit/naturepl.com, pp. 4, 11; © Peter Blackwell/naturepl.com, p. 5; © Beverly Joubert/National Geographic/Getty Images, p. 6; © Jan Tove Johansson/Taxi/Getty Images, p. 7; © Vincent Munier/naturepl.com, pp. 8, 18; © Manoj Shah/Stone/Getty Images, p. 9; © Tony Heald/naturepl.com, pp. 12, 15, 21, 28, 34; © Peter Johnson/CORBIS, p. 17; © Roger De La Harpe/ The Image Bank/Gallo Images/Getty Images, p. 22; © Pete Oxford/naturepl.com, p. 23; © Staffan Widstrand/CORBIS, p. 24; © Anup Shah/naturepl.com, p. 27; © Mitsuaki Iwago/Minden Pictures, p. 29; © Jeff Foott/naturepl.com, p. 30; © Mattias Klum/National Geographic/Getty Images, p. 31; © Peter Johnson/CORBIS, p. 33; © Nicola Jenner, p. 36; © ABPL/Gerald Hinde/Animals. Animals, p. 37. front cover: © Beverly Joubert/National Geographic/Getty Images. Back cover (top): © Beverly Joubert/National Geographic/Getty Images. Back cover (bottom): *Army Ants*: © Christian Ziegler; *Hyenas*: © Richard du Toit/naturepl.com; *Jackals*: © Beverly Joubert/National Geographic/Getty Images; *Tasmanian Devils*: Photodisc Royalty Free by Getty Images; *Vultures*: © Chris Hellier/ CORBIS; *Wolverines*: © Daniel J. Cox/naturalexposures.com.

Copyright © 2005 by Sandra Markle

All rights reserved. International copyright secured. No part of this book may be reproduced, stored in a retrieval system, or transmitted in any form or by any means—electronic, mechanical, photocopying, recording, or otherwise—without the prior written permission of Lerner Publications Company except for brief quotations in an acknowledged review.

Lerner Publications Company
A division of Lerner Publishing Company
241 First Avenue North
Minneapolis, MN 55401 U.S.A.

Website address: www.lernerbooks.com

Library of Congress Cataloging-in-Publication Data

Markle, Sandra.
    Jackals / by Sandra Markle.
      p.   cm. — (Animal scavengers)
    Includes bibliographical references and index.
    ISBN-13: 978−0−8225−3197−5 (lib. bdg. : alk. paper)
    ISBN-10: 0−8225−3197−6 (lib. bdg. : alk. paper)
    1. Jackals—Juvenile literature. I. Title. II. Series: Markle, Sandra. Animal scavengers.
  QL737.C22M3635 2005
  599.77'2—dc22   2004029672

Manufactured in the United States of America
1 2 3 4 5 6 − DP − 10 09 08 07 06 05

READ ANIMAL PREDATORS, A BOOKLIST TOP 10 YOUTH NONFICTION SERIES BY SANDRA MARKLE

Crocodiles
Great White Sharks
Killer Whales
Lions
Owls
Polar Bears
Wolves